Food for Thought

Duane Ashley Poole

authorHOUSE®

AuthorHouse™
1663 Liberty Drive
Bloomington, IN 47403
www.authorhouse.com
Phone: 1 (800) 839-8640

Published by AuthorHouse 01/08/2018

ISBN: 978-1-5462-2298-9 (sc)
ISBN: 978-1-5462-2297-2 (e)

Library of Congress Control Number: 2017919768

Print information available on the last page.

This book is printed on acid-free paper.

The Holy Bible, English Standard Version. ESV® Text Edition: 2016. Copyright © 2001 by Crossway Bibles, a publishing ministry of Good News Publishers.

Contents

———◆◆◆———

Introduction

———⬦⬦⬦———

Growing up I would listen to the lyrics of many hip hop and R&B songs, and I found this to be a therapeutic way of self-expression for myself. Whenever I felt inspired, I would throw on an instrumental track or some kind of backing beat, and I would start writing down my thoughts. Every time I wrote something down, I would put my writings inside a shoebox and thought nothing of them at the time.

Until, that is, I started to let other people read some of my verses and poems, and their positive feedback reaffirmed that I should continue writing whenever I felt inspired to do so.

One day later in life I checked my shoebox and realized I had enough material written down to create a book, and this became my goal—to get my writings published.

My inspiration for writing comes from various sources, including music, movies, books on religion and spirituality, and from reading about current world events in the newspapers.

I would say my style of writing is mostly influenced from hip hop verses, especially the rhyming aspect of it.

Both my mother and my grandmother are great creative writers too, and I am certain this is where my literary talent comes from. I hope you enjoy my book, *Food for Thought*!

To my family here in the United States of America and across the pond in England.

Only God can judge the living (comprehensive consciousness).

Comprehensive consciousness means a singular omnipotent (unlimited power), omniscient (infinite knowledge), and omnipresent (present everywhere) divine entity existing throughout the infinite universe, thus having unlimited perspective. This means only God himself can judge the living.

1

The Greater Glory of God (Miracles and Phenomena)

A miracle is Chesley Sullenberger landing an Airbus A320 on the Hudson River. Captain Sully's heroic feat saved everybody aboard the flight. What a legendary tale!

Fabrice Muamba, while a soccer player for the Bolton Wanderers, had a heart attack while playing against Tottenham Hotspur. Fabrice suffered a cardiac arrest and died for seventy-eight minutes after he collapsed on the pitch. It's unfathomable Fabrice survived and recovered. Halleluiah!

Gabrielle Giffords, a former congresswoman, was shot in the head at close range with a 9-millimeter semiautomatic pistol in Tucson, Arizona. It's a miracle she defied the odds and has since been on an astonishing road to recovery.

Miracles happen throughout the universe every day, yet many people shrug them off, putting them down to chance, luck, and coincidence.

A phenomenon is manifested through the lives of extraordinary people and their incredible talents.

A phenomenon is exhibited through Stevie Wonder. Although blind, he was a child prodigy and is now able to play a wide array of instruments.

I saw it in Tiger Woods, who sent the ball soaring through the sky, landing in the middle of the fairway.

I saw the phenomenon in Michael Jackson, who moved with awe-inspiring grace. It was like he walked across the stage on air while doing the moon walk, which was revered by the world.

I saw the phenomena in Michael Jordan's spectacular slam dunks, and I saw it in the great Muhammad Ali's shuffle.

I heard an angel or something of a phenomenon sing to us through the voice of Whitney Houston while she performed "The Star-Spangled Banner" at Super Bowl XXV.

I see the remnants of Steve Jobs's phenomenal ingenuity and innovation through the sophisticated gadgetry we enjoy today.

I learned of Martin Luther King Jr.'s awe-inspiring, phenomenal "I Have a Dream" speech. In retrospect, it speaks prophecy as in 2008, we had the first African American president, Barack Hussein Obama, who was reelected in 2012.

I see something phenomenal in the legacy of Albert Einstein. He left behind a gift with his special theory of relativity, and his deep imagination and intelligence have helped shape some of the finest technology we use in the twenty-first century.

Miracles and phenomena are all around us, and I believe they are more profound than we give them credit for.

I believe these countless miracles and phenomena bestowed upon us in the world are for the greater glory of God!

2

Intransigence

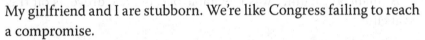

My girlfriend and I are stubborn. We're like Congress failing to reach a compromise.

She wants everything expensive, and she wants it right now!

I try to tell her it's not always in either party's best interest.

We go back and forth, like a Democrat and Republican.

I'm playing Bill Clinton, while she's playing Sarah Palin.

She's rather loquacious, constantly in my ear over all the partisanship.

I'm trying to balance our budget; she's adding to our deficit.

I'm a Democrat at heart, but when it comes to money, I'm a fiscal conservative.

I'm trying to be prudent and revive our economy, so we can build a brighter future together.

She wants Congress to pass a bill for her to spend more on what we don't need.

I'm trying to veto the bill so she can spend more in the future, but she must take some austerity measures now.

She's making poor choices when it comes to this war on debt, and as a result, we're paying the price of being downgraded.

I told her to cut spending, but she never listens, and then we start to argue over all our downsizing.

I'm losing a lot of sleep, worried sick about our future, so I asked Congress for more money I don't have.

Now I'm faced with a deadline to pay back the loan, trying to save both my relationship and our home.

I'm starting to be frugal with money, but she tells me to quit being cheap.

Next, we're exchanging verbal punches because we fail to make a deal.

The only option is to go our separate ways because my girlfriend's intransigent when it comes to spending money!

We try to work something out before the deadline comes knocking on our door.

Damn it; we're too stubborn to get things done and sign off on anything.

Before we break up, we decide to go out for one last drive.

A financial calamity was inevitable because she drove us off the fiscal cliff!

3

From Tragedy to Triumph (Stay Strong)

Every day's a battle when you go to school and you have to contend with being tormented at recess.

Your only crime is being a genius in class, and your contemporaries ridicule you for it.

You go home with bottled-up emotions, feeling humiliated and dreading the thought of facing another day filled with mental and physical cruelty.

All your class bullies post inappropriate pictures of you on Facebook so other people can laugh at your expense.

A dark cloud has suddenly come over you, and all the misery you face every day has finally taken its toll.

You are in a dire need of a sign because you cannot see anything in life getting any better.

You start to hear voices in your mind, urging you to give up.

Hope for you seems like an illusion, and you are never going to see a brighter day again.

The truth is you are special, and your best years lie ahead of you!

Nothing lasts forever—neither good nor bad—and if you fight the war long enough, then great things will ensue in the future or you.

Talk to the people closest in your life, and you will find a solution to circumvent your situation.

Nothing is as bad as it seems; there's a way around most problems.

Focus on being the genius you are; your future is bright if you can muster the strength to make it past the troubling times you are going through.

If you give up, you will cut short all the great things that await you in your life.

Stay strong and survive, and you will transition from tragedy to triumph. And in the future, you will look back on the days you were bullied and rejoice at the fact that you made it through your darkest hour. You will smile again, and the dark cloud that once encompassed you will be lifted.

4

Too Much Too Soon (Transience)

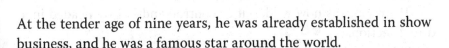

At the tender age of nine years, he was already established in show business, and he was a famous star around the world.

His lifestyle was a novelty to him at first, but in life, it's good to have a happy medium because everything in excess gets old fast.

He had the money, fame, and all of the assets that came with being a celebrity.

His parents were proud of him because he had all the adulation and accolades that most people dream of.

He was once a fresh-faced young star adored by everyone in the world, and his merchandise was available from every major retail outlet.

He was growing up fast before the media, and he was living a fairy-tale life.

But once he hit twenty-one years of age, his life started to spiral out of control; he was in the headlines of every national newspaper, drifting away from the clean-cut image he once portrayed.

Drugs became his new venture as he grew tired of the fame, traveling overseas, and he became enraged with the paparazzi watching his every move.

He started to take everything he had for granted, and he experienced so much in life at such a young age that nothing was exciting to him anymore.

Every day in the media you would see pictures of him staggering out of nightclubs after a binge, looking worse for wear.

He had the beautiful girls, fast cars, and big mansions, but it was like he was seeking something else in life that simply was not there.

Every time the paparazzi came to take pictures of him, he would verbally and physically assault them, and he tried to smash their cameras.

He used to love signing his autograph for his fans, but now he was in the press for taking his frustration out on them.

He was now hard into heroin and cocaine, and he started to knock on death's door from all the drugs he indulged in.

His parents tried to intervene on their son's behalf on numerous occasions, but it was all to no avail.

Their son was now wild, out of control, and swiftly headed in a dire direction.

When he was twenty-five years of age, his addiction finally took its toll, and he took a combination of drugs mixed with alcohol that rendered him unconscious, and doctors placed him in a medically induced coma.

Every day his parents remained vigilant by their son's bedside, hoping and praying for him to have a miracle recovery.

But on one sad day, their hopes vanished when the doctors walked in and told them their son was brain dead, and there was nothing else they could do for him.

His distraught and inconsolable family had no choice but to pull the plug on him, and he died just before his twenty-sixth birthday.

He was such an icon that when the headline news read he had passed away from a drug overdose, it sent shockwaves around the globe.

He was a young heartthrob who affected and touched many lives around the world, and it felt surreal to many of his fans that at such a young age, he was now deceased.

5

The Luck of the Irish

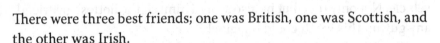

There were three best friends; one was British, one was Scottish, and the other was Irish.

All three made a bet when they were at school together about who was going to have the biggest house, the most ostentatious vehicle, and the prettiest girlfriend.

The British and the Scottish friend were both academically adept, and they always scored in the 90 percent ratio on each and every one of their tests.

The Irish friend was a slacker in school, always getting poor grades, and he never really took anything seriously.

The British and the Scottish friends excluded their Irish counterpart from the bet they all had pledged together, feeling as though he had no chance of attaining their widely talked about success in the future.

The British and the Scottish friends both finished high school with honors, while the Irish friend dropped out without any qualifications.

The British friend found the job market scarce, so he took his first job as a laborer in the construction field.

The Scottish friend found getting a job hard as well, but he managed to get some work in a factory producing furniture.

The Irish friend found no work at all, so he immediately went on the dole.

The British and the Scottish friends worked arduously every day in their jobs.

They both said to their Irish friend on the dole, "You have no chance at winning the bet all three of us pledged at school!"

The Irish friend played the lottery religiously, and on one occasion, he checked his numbers while watching the drawing on television, and to his amazement, he matched every single number.

The Irish friend won a staggering ten million pounds on the lottery! He had a chuckle to himself, knowing clearly he had won the bet.

As soon as the Irish friend redeemed his payout at the official lottery claims center, he bought a nice house worth just under a million pounds. He also treated himself to an exclusive luxury BMW vehicle. Not only that, but he also scored himself the hottest girlfriend any guy on this earth could imagine!

The British and Scottish friends both asked God, "How could this happen? We scored good grades in our exams at school, and we both toiled every day at work, to no avail."

The Irish friend smirked at his British and Scottish friends, saying to them both, "Don't take it personally, but I was blessed since birth with one thing you two don't have."

The British and Scottish friends both asked, "So what makes you so special?"

The Irish friend flashed a big, smug grin, and said, "I was born with the luck of the Irish."

6

The Clairvoyant

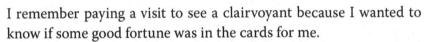

I remember paying a visit to see a clairvoyant because I wanted to know if some good fortune was in the cards for me.

The thoughts on my present circumstances were very bleak, and that's all I could imagine—nothing ever changing.

I discussed how I felt with the clairvoyant about my incessant negative thinking.

She gave me some profound wisdom and good advice, and I couldn't help but smile like Don King waving his American flag.

She told me, "Too much thinking is making life more complex than it is. Focus solely on what's important, and try not to compare your circumstances to other people or you will never find true happiness. People often become disillusioned with life when our dreams do not materialize the way we imagined they would. Always keep your spirit invigorated, and quit thinking about the continuum in life because I see great things happening for you in the future."

The clairvoyant told me not to let my mind wander and think so much about worldly objects.

She told me life would take me to places I couldn't imagine myself ever seeing if only I gave it a chance.

She said, "Things will work out in time, and all the trivial things that once bothered you in your youth will become insignificant in the future. Know that reality TV is a poisonous manipulator of perception, trying to shift your ideals onto material things instead of spiritual ones."

My clairvoyant told me, "Don't be quick to become despondent, and carry on living a balanced harmonious life. There are some great things coming that you can't fathom right now, but most importantly know you will always have enough to suffice."

7

Thoughts Worth Living For

I am a visionary, seeing the picture in my mind way in advance.

I summon my imagination and all of its wonderful contents.

My faith never wanes, even though wishes can take a while to materialize.

Negativity seeks a way into my mind using deceit, but I refute such thoughts.

My dreams never fade. I always keep them in the back of my mind.

I know a change will come because I'm stubborn and persistent.

Never am I discouraged by the time it takes for me to rendezvous with destiny.

I am still for the Lord, waiting patiently for a rainbow to appear when I least expect it.

Nothing stands in my way because I will circumvent any obstacle until I reach my utopia.

I'll wait with patience and contentment for my innermost desires.

I won't become a skeptic or doubtful of what is sure to come.

I want my thoughts and all I am thinking to manifest into the physical world.

You see, these thoughts are so magnificent that they alone are worth living for!

8

Fakebook

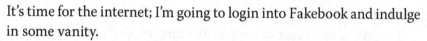

It's time for the internet; I'm going to login into Fakebook and indulge in some vanity.

I have over a thousand friends I'm constantly trying to outdo and impress.

In order to do this, I have to constantly update my profile and post the most transcendent pictures possible.

Now get ready for all the narcissism I'm going to project on my page.

Look at me outside Buckingham palace posing with the queen's guard.

I'm oblivious to all the troubles of the world; this is my special domain of solace.

All I am concerned about is my wild escapades and how many people add a nice comment to my pictures.

I have just logged in to check my messages, when I notice some new friend requests.

Oh, I remember they're some old school pals I've not seen or heard from in years.

Maybe they're being nosey, trying to see what I am doing with my life!

I guess they will be pleased with my holiday brochure; I have visited over a thousand cities throughout the world.

They can see me in various photos, especially the ones of me in New York, Paris, and London.

Bet you these captivating pictures will inspire and leave a solid impression on all my rivals.

I wonder why my new friends have not spoken or left any new comments on my adventures.

I'm starting to get perturbed by all these phonies not having the courtesy to send me a note.

Maybe they're jealous and envy my lifestyle; after all, I have been around the world three times and back!

Despite the abysmal economy and all the troubles in the world, everybody is perceived as doing fine.

Especially me. Look at my profile—you wouldn't know the world's in total and utter chaos.

When it's my birthday or any special occasion, you best believe I'm celebrating in style.

I don't care if my credit cards are maxed out and my bills are all overdue.

I'll do anything to capture the most glorious picture in order to ooze with pride and gratification.

Look at me in Sin City popping a bottle of the finest champagne in town.

I'll endure leaps and bounds to spice up my profile and pretend about my status.

If you want to engross yourself in a genre of fantasy, then go to Fakebook, sign up, and log in.

Prepare to enter a realm of superficiality, and get acquainted with a thousand best enemies!

9

Life's Like a Game of Poker!

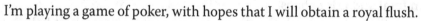

I'm playing a game of poker, with hopes that I will obtain a royal flush.

Life is a future road without precognition, and sometimes I wonder what's in the cards.

The game of life can be difficult when you're constantly dealt a high card or one pair.

I'm trying to conquer my problems, and I have just been dealt a four of a kind.

I know with this hand I'll have a pretty good opportunity to seize the moment.

All my rivals are trying to read me using their intuition from previous experiences.

Everybody's objective is the same. We're all in the game of life to try and win.

With this in mind, I'll hold onto hope and not be too quick to fold!

I know I'm in with a chance, and I'm thinking to myself all my opponents must be bluffing.

It's unlikely they have a straight flush, let alone a royal flush, so I'll stick to my guns for now.

I had confidence in my body language and overall disposition.

That's when I went ahead and raised everybody $100,000.

Everybody folded apart from one stubborn rival, who raised me on my offer.

I became a little anxious because I knew there was a possibility of him having a better hand.

I almost succumbed to my nerves, but then I had a conscience telling me, "Don't be too quick to yield."

That's when I grabbed hold of my chips, and said, "I'm going all in!"

My opponent put down a straight flush over my four of a kind.

I lost out on the grand prize this time around, but I know my four of a kind could have easily been a royal flush.

You see, life is like a game of poker, and there's hope as long as we are playing the cards of life we are dealt.

This is the driving force behind my tenacity, and I remain optimistic that one day my cards will be the winners!

10

Through the Eyes of a Child

———◆◆◆———

I came into this world without knowledge, pure of heart, and everything about me was innocent.

When I first opened my eyes, I saw the world how it was supposed to be seen in a natural light.

Its thirty years later, and since that moment in time, unnatural occurrences subsequently followed.

Hatred, racism, and the difference of ideology that have always existed throughout society inevitably led me to sin.

Down the road, certain experiences in life deceived my mind and led me astray.

Society and miscellaneous influences can have a tendency of changing one's perspective.

I can walk my own path using my own discernment, or I can succumb to the temptation of societal pressure.

I live in a polarized society, and this very divisiveness is often the cause of conflict that can bring about an array of intense emotions.

Many times I feel rage and indignation, but then I understand the fact we are all sinners born into a cruel and wicked world.

I used to have a quick temper, and I would react to things out of anger before I could manage to rationalize my thoughts.

I always had eyes but couldn't quite see the bigger picture, so now I forgive a person for what is unnatural.

It's the blind leading the blind, and we are all corrupted by vice and sin.

The world can be overwhelming at times, and it's easy to get caught up in all the darkness that goes around!

You can let the evils of the world influence your mind, permeating your soul to the point of feeling lost and troubled.

Or you can see through the eyes of a child and witness perfection in an imperfect world.

When you see through the eyes of a child, you'll realize everything impure is a fallacy.

When you see through the eyes of a child, you will realize hatred is not a reality.

11

Life Is Suspenseful

———— ✦ ————

The suspense of life has me sitting on the edge of my seat, making me anxious when I picture a future filled with great mystery and uncertainty.

Life is suspenseful, like a game of basketball, especially when both teams go all the way down to the wire and you're unsure which team will be victorious when the game is all said and done.

Life is not about how we start or what advantages another person had over us. It's all about how we end up in the future.

Life to me is a riveting novel that has me deeply engrossed from chapter to chapter.

I remember reading about a homeless beggar on the streets who didn't know where his next meal was coming from.

The next thing you know, he did a good deed, and his story was so compelling that donors from all across America wanted to help him out of his dire situation.

One minute he was homeless on the streets living rough, without a dollar to his name, but now he's a proud homeowner thanks to all the donors and the people who raised money for him.

We don't know how our lives are going to materialize, and that's when I think about the pizza delivery man Edgar Martirosyan who ended up on live television in front of millions of viewers during the 2014 Oscar's ceremony. Edgar Martirosyan subsequently went on to receive a thousand-dollar tip and is probably selling more pizzas now than ever before!

When I walk down the street, I can see the path ahead of me, but I don't know what's lurking around the corner.

The anticipation of a good life unfolding reinvigorates me and gives me strength to continue on fighting for my hopes and dreams.

In life I have been lost inside plenty of dark mazes, and I often wondered at times how I would ever get out of the darkness I found myself in.

But then a new day arrived, giving me the light I needed to guide me out of the dark maze and get me back to square one again.

You see, life is a game full of suspense, and I'm sitting in my courtside seat intrigued on how my game will unfold.

12

Faces Tell a Story

———————◆◆◆◆———————

I remember sitting in the middle of town enjoying a cup of coffee outside a local café. As I was sipping my coffee, I started observing people from all walks of life going about their business. I was looking at various facial expressions, and in a moment of time, I had a clairvoyant experience, seeing how people's faces can tell a story. I started to look beyond the faces I saw, and then I incorporated a stroke of my own perception. I noticed one woman walking through town, and she had a glowing and smooth complexion. She looked rather vivacious, and I could tell she came from a good family with a good support mechanism. She looked well rested, and I could see that life at this point was treating her well. I observed a second woman, and her face projected a different story. I could see the pain and stress in her weathered face, and when I looked at her eyes, they told me a story of worry, concern, anxiety, and restlessness. Her hair was disheveled, and I could tell she had the weight of the world on her shoulders! I could see a picture of this woman working hard, getting inadequate sleep, and struggling financially. Unlike the first woman, life didn't seem to be treating the second woman very well. As she passed me, we both made eye contact, and this is when I gave her a nod with a warm and kind smile, hoping this simple gesture of kindness would mitigate her pain and make her day a little bit brighter. Sometimes our busy lifestyles keep us unaware of people's pain and suffering. If we can take one brief moment in time out of our busy lifestyle to give a kind word or gesture, a small act of grace can make all the difference.

13

Planting the Seeds of Good Karma

———◇◇◇◇◇———

I'm coming across various people in the neighborhood, and they each have their own set of circumstances.

What I do for these people will determine the outcome of my karma, so I'm planting my best seeds possible.

I came across somebody in the community, and he needed some gas money so he could get back and forth to work for the rest of the week.

Many other people ignored this man's plight despite being able to help him out with his situation.

I, on the other hand, refused to ignore his predicament, so I loaned him the money he needed, enabling him to get through the week.

After I lent him the money, he was ever so gracious, and he showed me his utmost gratitude.

When I went out a week later and checked my mailbox, I noticed a thank-you note from my neighbor, and he paid me back, doubling the money I lent him.

The other people who ignored the man and his situation did not reap anything, for what they planted was nothing.

I, however, set my harvest in motion, and in return I received a blessing from the Holy Spirit.

There were quite a few people out in the community who all needed a good turn and a good deed from somebody.

I believe we're all serving a unique purpose, and we can help out our fellowman with a simple act of kindness.

Most people out in the community needed a financial blessing, so I gave to them whatever I could afford.

The people who I gave to were ever so thankful, and their appreciation alone was more than reciprocation.

Many people in the community did not understand the give to God seed principle, and so many fell short with their harvest.

I, however, planted a multitude of seeds, and I scattered my good deeds all throughout the community.

It is better to give than to receive, and I helped many people with their situation simply through doing a good turn in their time of need.

When I awoke one morning, my harvest was bountiful, just as I imagined.

I served my community well, and I was able to give even more generously to others who needed a financial blessing.

I reaped what I sowed in the community, and good karma was coming back around my way.

I planted my seeds of good karma through doing what was noble by the people in the neighborhood.

You see, my acts of benevolence had a boomerang effect because the good karma I put into the universe came back to me tenfold!

14

Las Vegas (Surreal City)

———————◆◆◆◆◆———————

Soon as I entered the Las Vegas Airport, I was immediately beckoned by the allure of all the many different slot machines.

It takes strength of character to resist the temptation of blowing all your money as soon as you touch down in Vegas!

I caught a taxi to Caesars Palace, and as I was riding toward my destination, I could not help but be awe inspired!

I marveled at seeing legendary fighters up on the billboards, and the vast array of hotels standing sumptuously in the middle of a desert.

I immersed myself into the bright lights, and it felt harmonious to mingle with various people from all around the world.

I clocked the Eiffel Tower, Statue of Liberty, Egyptian pyramids, and all the astounding worldly architecture.

As I pulled up and arrived inside Caesar's Palace, I could not believe such opulence and grandeur manifested inside this hotel building.

I checked in, and the bellhop carried my bags up to my suite. I gave the bellhop a tip and sprawled across the bed in total relaxation.

After getting some shut-eye, I felt refreshed and knew there was a lot on the agenda, such as eating the best dishes from all corners of the world, gambling, shows, and art. You are so spoiled for entertainment!

So I showered, freshened myself up, fixed myself a drink, and threw on some nice clothes.

Before leaving, I made sure I had my room key, and then I took the elevator down to star level and smiled at the regality in which I was staying.

I walked toward the strip, and the entrepreneurial spirit was vibrant. The city was sprawling with people from all around the world.

I admired the water show and the elation on people's faces outside the front of Caesar's Palace.

I couldn't help but think, *It's such a blessing to be alive. Now let the good times commence in surreal city.*

15

The Fraternity (Survival)

————◈————

The fraternity comes together in fellowship, sharing and splitting money in order to survive through these tough economic times.

I formed an alliance similar to a brotherhood, and we help each other maintain throughout the struggle as best we can.

Nothing in the world appears to be sacred anymore. A lot of professions are feeling the pinch due to state and federal cuts.

My meager salary is no longer enough to sustain me autonomously, and this is why I formed the fraternity: we can all empathize with the extortionate cost of living.

My group is constructive, each member serving a purpose, so we're able to weather the storm and make it through as best we can.

My friends come together to discuss the rent money, as we can no longer buy houses due to banks tightening up their lending processes to folks with bad credit.

My club no longer goes to the grocery store to buy meat. We go hunting instead, and we bring back enough venison to feed a multitude of families.

The fraternity does everything to make life a little less stressful, and we all chip in with the utility bills so we have enough for luxuries, including overpriced rental movies.

I used to see the wife and husband go out to work, and their combined wages would see them through each and every month.

Now I'm seeing couples doubling and even tripling their living arrangements in order to meet their monthly requirements.

I see people building alliances through friendship, and I'm seeing so many people live under one roof it reminds me of a frat house. Basic items such as a loaf of bread, eggs, milk, and cheese are skyrocketing to the point where the average Joe Blow is being forced out of the market, and so people are forming unions like the fraternity.

Capitalism is in a downward spiral due to the shortage of good-paying jobs and timid consumer spending.

People are mostly spending their money on necessities, and small business enterprises are closing as fast as they open.

The digital age of ordering everything online is making jobs in the private sector scarce, so we help each other to find jobs by networking via social media if anybody gets made redundant.

I have organized and formed a club called the fraternity, and we come together collectively sharing our monthly expenditures, all in the name of survival!

16

I'm all Right, Jack! (Sarcasm)

———⬦———

I'm a monumental corporation, and I'm so influential, I can get laws passed through legislation.

I don't care about the next man's struggles because I have been a lucrative entity since I was born.

My only concern is making the poor poorer and the rich richer.

I'm the master of manipulating revenue in my favor through having a product in high demand.

The only thing on my mind is capitalism and capital gains, basically anything where I'm profiteering.

I'm living high on the hog, looking down on the man lying in the street, as if he's not important!

I'm responsible for people suffering in silence with their ailments because my treatment is unaffordable!

I am very greedy and self-centered, only looking at things from my own limited perspective.

My attitude is if I can drive in my brand new Porsche, then surely you can too.

I have forgotten about my upbringing and how I had access to all the best opportunities.

I have a smug personality, relishing in the thought of checking my new bank balance.

Who cares about the gap widening between the rich and the poor? I certainly couldn't care less.

I have total apathy for everybody who does not belong in the category of the 1 percent.

It's a rich man's world, and if you cannot keep up with the game of life, then shame on you.

I'm ruthless and selfish to the point you can witness me salivating for my next big paycheck.

Inflations don't bother me. I'm all for deregulation and free enterprise.

Everybody's out for self in today's society, and I'm all right, Jack, is the motto we follow!

17

The Miracle Pill

———◇◇◇◇◇———

One night I had a dream about a group of scientists who all had enhanced genes from selective breeding.

They worked together collectively, and between them, they discovered the miracle pill.

This was a singular pill that would eradicate many illnesses and diseases known to all of humanity.

Many bereaved families whose loved ones would lose their battle from the wicked, insidious nature of cancer were being saved through taking this miracle pill.

Children were no longer being taken from this life too soon, leaving inconsolable parents due to this incredible pill!

Alzheimer's and dementia would be a thing of the past.

Families were no longer dealing with the terrible burden of looking after patients who could no longer recognize them.

The strain of watching a person twenty four hours a day incase their loved ones wondered away unnoticed, and not being able to leave their homes unassisted would be obliterated by this wonderful pill.

The miracle pill was a beneficial discovery for all of the human race, and the mortality rate for the average man and woman was ninety years of age.

An estimated one in five Americans are suffering with some form of mental health disorder. That's 43.8 million Americans afflicted from this terrible illness in a given year.

Imagine you are suffering from severe depression due to a chemical imbalance of the brain, and you are about to do something tragic.

The miracle pill would act as a savior for anyone suffering from mental illness because you can take it and be completely nullified from wanting to do yourself or anyone else harm.

I had a dream the miracle pill was a remarkable discovery for people suffering from their many different ailments, and many who are suffering and the many tragedies caused by these illnesses would be no more.

18

Chicago Laments

———————————◆◈◆———————————

There are many young souls in the windy city so full of promise and so full of potential.

But the environment in which these young children live is not conducive to their safety or cognitive development because all they see is bloodshed and violence.

Many of these kids have good souls and want nothing more than to succeed in life and go to school to get a good education, only they are too afraid to leave their houses in order to get to where they need to go.

They are victims of their circumstances, trapped in a world where people are being gunned down simply for being in the wrong place at the wrong time.

There are many young teenage boys who want to participate in social activities such as basketball with their friends, and they all share their common dreams of becoming the next Michael Jordan.

However, they have lost so many of their friends and family members to senseless gun crime that they're all afraid of becoming the next victim so their life becomes one of fear and avoidance.

Living in the tough inner city of Chicago will have a devastating impact on the psyche of the youth, and many will go on to suffer from a list of mental health disorders.

Many people will be pressured and forced into becoming

something they are not, and this will end with them having a criminal record before their lives have even begun.

This ultimately impedes the chances of many young men who had dreams and aspirations to thrive and excel in the world.

Now that they have criminal records, their opportunities have become fewer, and they will most likely become recidivists.

There are many flowers waiting to bloom and blossom into something majestic if only their environment would allow them to be safe and secure when they walk down the streets.

There are many kids who have dreams larger than life itself, but it's so unfortunate and tragic when a bullet with no name snatches the precious light away from a child whose dreams will no longer manage to materialize.

19

The Dreamer and the Realist

———❖———

The dreamer thinks big, and sometimes other people find them peculiar for their unconventional way of thinking.

The realist sees things for what they are, and when the dreamer shares his hopes and ambitions, the realist shrugs them off as if their desires will never come true.

They often get mocked, laughed at, and ridiculed for trying to obtain the type of success a realist finds impractical.

In most cases, the dreamer fails to achieve the unimaginable, and this only reinforces the realist's worldview.

Although the odds of succeeding are stacked heavily against them, they don't let this discourage them, for they are very courageous and tenacious people.

The realists of the world quickly adapt to the situation at hand, and they just get on with what they think is feasible.

But when the dreamer's obstinacy pays off with flying colors, his or her success often galvanizes the doubters into becoming more open minded.

Because the dreamers' achievements inspire and prove to the realists that if you work hard enough and never give up, then any dreams you have can certainly become a reality!

20

Dystopia

I see countries like Venezuela as the harbinger for a dystopian-like future to arise among a percentage of the free world.

You see the rich are enjoying themselves, indulging in all of their pleasures while everybody else is living in misery and squalor.

Lawlessness abounds to the point that kidnappings for ransom money are a daily occurrence because predators are preying on defenseless families, and the police are nothing more than redundant.

Hospitals are becoming a health hazard without basic supplies, and the once-solid middle class is in the streets scavenging for food.

The humanitarian crisis is so dire that there is nothing on the shelves of any grocery stores, and everyone apart from the rich is starving.

Poor, emaciated animals locked up in rundown zoos are a common sight to see around the world.

War, famine, and pestilence are out of control, and antibiotics are an antiquated antidote for many diseases.

Life is like the movie called *The Purge*, and governments cannot help us, so it's every man for himself.

The world is so out of control that the rich and the elite have absconded to their personal islands patrolled twenty-four–seven by their own unique security.

Meanwhile the 99 percent are so hungry they are eating anything, including rats, in order to survive.

Most nations are so insolvent that vulnerable people who were once entitled to benefits are no longer receiving them, and because of colossal cuts to social services, many people with disabilities are dying even in the most advanced countries.

Homelessness and displaced people are a common occurrence because housing is no longer affordable.

I read about the zika virus in Brazil or another of its kind cascading to the point that viruses have become an unsustainable global pandemic.

All the signs around the world point toward the last days according to biblical prophecy; the world as we know it is doomed!

21

Schizophrenia (God Is with You)

I used to think life had no particular meaning or purpose because I couldn't fathom anything beyond this earthly realm.

You see lately, my mind has been racing, and I keep receiving subliminal signs, as if an invisible agent is trying to subtly correspond with me.

I turned on the TV this morning, and there was a pastor preaching on some religious channel.

Normally I would change the channel, but I stayed glued to every word this pastor spoke, as if he was literally talking to me through a divine spirit.

Every time I read some literature and listen to the words of a song, it feels as if the words are inadvertently describing something concerning my life.

It's hard for me to distinguish the reality from fantasy, and it's like I am constantly dueling with two personalities.

I feel like I am on the edge, tapping into a part of my mind that is devoid from the people who are sane, and nobody can understand me.

I remember walking down the street one day in a state of apprehension, reading all the sign postings and billboards.

As I kept looking up and reading the billboards, I stumbled across one that felt exclusive to me for some uncanny reason.

The billboard read out in big bold letters, "Don't worry, and don't let your heart be troubled, for God is with you!

22

Agoraphobia

———————◇◈◇———————

So many troubles abound in the world today, and it's getting to the point where I don't want to leave my house anymore.

Every time I pick up the newspaper and read the headlines, you would think the second coming of Christ is imminent.

The immigration crisis throughout Europe and its loose borders have attracted a pernicious undercurrent of crime and terrorism.

Whenever I muster up enough courage to walk to my local ATM machine, I take my two big Rottweilers with me!

My anxiety and paranoid thoughts that people are conspiring to plot against me without warrant has me feeling vulnerable, so I am always cautious and vigilant.

I used to be confident in myself, but the city in which I live in has become alarmingly dangerous.

With all the government cuts taking place, the police presence in the area has significantly diminished.

This problem only makes the criminals more brazen to carry out their attacks with impunity.

I used to go out in public looking dapper in appearance, until I kept on attracting shady-looking drug addicts who always begged me for some loose change.

Now when I do pluck up the courage to venture out, I merely blend in with a foretelling dystopian society.

If I had all the money in the world to sustain me for the rest of my natural life, I would make my own home a utopian paradise so I could feel at ease with my anxieties on the world and current agoraphobia.

23

Perspective

———————◆◆◆◆———————

One day I walked into town and saw a homeless man talking in riddles. He was a man who appeared to be afflicted with severe mental illness.

I remember one time speaking with a vet who served in both Afghanistan and Iraq telling me he lost his limbs when he stepped on an IED, and now he has to wear prosthetic legs and arms.

One time when I visited the hospital, I met an eleven-year-old girl who told me she had terminal cancer with only a few months to live.

I started to appreciate my family more because I thought of the homeless man who had nobody battling his mental illness all alone on the streets.

I admired the fortitude and resolve of the wounded warrior I met because despite his condition, he had the most positive demeanor about him.

Sometimes I take my life and health for granted, complaining and moaning over trivial matters.

Then I thought of the poor eleven-year-old girl with terminal cancer because her young precious life put everything into perspective!

24

Originals and Duplicates (Be Yourself)

There are originals who set trends with unique ideas that duplicates both admire and despise at the same time.

Duplicates love to copy the swag of a person with originality because duplicates love the word *plagiarism*.

Duplicates covet the style, charisma and leadership of the originals.

When you do something special with your life, you leave an indelible mark for duplicates to follow.

Originals leave the blueprint for success, and duplicates love to copy, as if they were the first ones to do it.

There are two types of people, followers and leaders.

Followers tend to do whatever the crowd is doing, but leaders have a vision for success, and they stick to the script until they achieve greatness.

Originals set the tone, and all the duplicates follow suit, trying to emulate what has already been done.

When you're the first person with a great idea, be careful not to reveal your hand because duplicates will steal your concept and try to claim the word *original*.

A duplicate uses an original as a prototype to try and leverage a stolen idea.

The original is a leader, and all the followers feed off of his energy.

The key to being original is just be yourself, and project to the world your own unique identity.

25

Off to the Bar (Escapism)

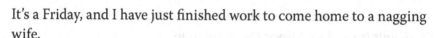

It's a Friday, and I have just finished work to come home to a nagging wife.

I'm tired of reality, so I'm off to the local bar to try to escape my troubles.

As I'm walking down the street, all kinds of madness is racing through my mind.

I can't seem to get ahead in life. These mountainous bills are a thorn in my side.

I'm trying my hardest to work within my set parameters, but my best never seems quite good enough.

These thoughts are so intense because I'm slogging my guts out, only to make pennies at the end of the week.

I have a credit card that needs paying down, but it seems a futile attempt when I'm only scratching off the interest.

All these real-life issues are taking their toll on my sanity; it must be so nice to be able to bend it like Beckham and make a fortune!

After a bitter thought process, I finally enter my local bar, where I can have a chat and a drink with my friends.

Dear bartender, keep them coming until all of my thoughts, and my imagination start bending the rules of reality.

I want to feel loose, carefree, and wild, until I'm numb to all of my worries.

This is my outlet and a temporary escape from all that's going on in my life.

I feel some solace knowing my friend I'm drinking with has problems similar to mine.

At least it lets me know I am not alone, and I'm sure there are plenty of others all in the same boat.

I keep the bartender busy pouring those drinks as I keep knocking them back one by one.

When the drink finally hits my head, I feel liberated, like all my problems have finally gone out the window.

Me and my friends shoot some pool and exchange some decent conversation, trying to savor the moment!

Time passes by fast, and the bartender rings the bell to let us all know that it's last call.

I buy the last round for my friends, and we quickly drown our sorrows before heading home to sleep.

Deep down I don't want this moment to cease because I know all that awaits me when I get home—an everlasting nagging wife who wants a holiday, and bills scattered all over the floor.

Closing time came around quick, and I'm out the door, staggering to the nearest takeaway for a curry.

After ordering my food, I head home with my takeout, looking forward to it absorbing all the alcohol I just consumed.

I eat my food and pass out on the couch, sleeping solidly until the rise of a Saturday afternoon.

Once awake, I have a splitting headache, a sore throat, and plenty of bills greeting me in the hallway.

I tried to escape from reality, but Groundhog Day is a very persistent part of life!

26

Transition of the Mind

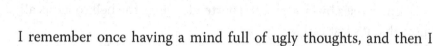

I remember once having a mind full of ugly thoughts, and then I made a transition when my thoughts became more beautiful than a northern cardinal bird.

You see, whenever I'm in a state of melancholy, I keep on fighting until I make a transition from misery to paradise.

I recall switching my gloomy thoughts of gray overcast to thinking about clear Caribbean blue skies.

My eyes went from taking nature for granted to appreciating the meticulous design behind the fur and skin coats of leopards, Bengal tigers, zebras, and many other incredible animals.

I went from thinking about the murky waters of Louisiana after the BP spill to thinking about Hawaiian, Tahitian, and Fiji waters.

My mind transitioned from heavy rain, fog, and blizzards to the sun coming out and rejuvenating my spirit.

I have to nourish my mind with new information, experiences, and activities or my thoughts and attitude become sullen.

My mind made the transition from a state of moroseness into the picturesque imagery of the Lake District located in the northwest of England.

Within my mind, I turned a deficient, decaying bridge into a highly structured fluorescent rainbow.

You see, the mind is a very complex tool, and in these hard times filled with volatility, I have to manage to block out the chaos by welcoming a brighter perspective.

So whenever I'm caught up in the madness and all the stressors of life, I realize it's crucial to make a positive transition of the mind through having a variety of sublime thoughts that will override all the negativity!

27

My Dream for Africa (Peace and Equality)

———————◇◆◇———————

One day many great leaders with the spirit of Nelson Mandela were born throughout the continent of Africa.

They were leaders of honor, respect, and integrity, and they stood by these core principles and virtues.

They stood up for the oppressed no matter what, and their hearts were never swayed by greed or anything materialistic in the world.

These leaders set a standard for Africa, and their vision for equality and prosperity reverberated throughout the continent.

They set such an example that every future incumbent followed suit to maintain their vision.

These new leaders despised anything rogue or corrupt and wanted to bury the hatchet of their predecessors once and for all.

All of the leaders across the continent of Africa formed a coalition, and they worked hard together to build a strong democracy for Africa.

They rendered all foreign aid for economic, humanitarian relief and made sure partisan politics would not stand in their way.

Knowledge and internet access even in the most remote places in Africa became so pervasive that people were able to start up small businesses for themselves.

Agriculture development in Africa helped people advance through climate change and droughts.

Everything was slow evolving, but the kids in the villages were no longer malnourished or dying from famine.

Everything had systematically changed for the better. Laws were enforced, and everyone had peace and equality.

Rebels, pirates, and militia men facilitating human trafficking and terrorism were being brought to justice.

The leaders started using their own natural resources, generating all kinds of revenue for the betterment of humanity.

They built pipelines and refineries for their oil, diamonds, and gold and then started to trade with the rest of the world.

Africa was the new market, and the people were no longer living with the depiction of starvation, deprivation, or hopelessness.

Entrepreneurs, business tycoons, great thinkers, and innovators all wanted to invest and bring their enterprises overseas.

Millions and millions of jobs were being created, and people throughout the continent were contributing to society.

Construction work was booming as the leaders invested funds into building their infrastructure and roads.

Africa became great, and people from all across the planet wanted to move there and live the dream.

Children of Africa who excelled in sports were coming to the forefront with their talents in great numbers.

Opportunity became vibrant, and people from all walks of life were flourishing across the continent of Africa.

Stock markets around the world started doing exceptionally well as Africa started to thrive.

All personal avarice and tyranny were completely obsolete, and the people continued to live happily and prosperous in my dream for Africa.

28

Unity after the Storm

———◆◆◆———

An Oklahoma tornado came through, hitting hard and devastating a whole community.

The aftermath of the EF-5 tornado destroyed a town and did more than $2 billion of damage.

I saw a natural disaster turn homes, schools, and places of leisure completely to rubble.

But what I admired most was the spirit after the tornado did its damage.

People rallied around, helping others in their time of great distress, searching for bodies of loved ones trapped beneath all the debris and rubble.

Everyone came together in the community, looking out for one another like family.

Teachers sacrificed their lives selflessly to save their students in the midst of extraordinary danger.

I read about strangers helping their fellowmen who were trapped beneath the rubble get from under it safely.

People from across the country pledged donations in support of the recovery from devastation.

I noticed something in the community that inspired me, and I knew there was a lot of good left despite all the evil we hear frequenting the news.

The Oklahoman spirit was second to none and time is no remedy, but as it moves on, so will the people!

Throughout the bereavement, suffering, and sorrow, I'm pretty sure the people of Oklahoma will rebuild their communities, and brighter days will hopefully follow.

But overall I was proud to see people helping one another out the best way they could, and these great acts of benevolence are everything I'm sure God intended for our lost and troubled world.

29

Channels of the Mind (Introspection)

◆━━━━━◈◆◈━━━━━◆

I tuned into the news channel, and my mood become exacerbated by all the suffering being reported around the world all day.

After I tuned into a comedy channel to try to lighten things up, that's when the humor of the comedian put a great deal of joy and laughter into my heart. You see, my mentality has to change channels to balance out the madness of life.

I caught up with an old friend, and we tuned into a history channel reminiscing on old times and feeling a sense of nostalgia. When we were conversing, I felt good taking a ride back down memory lane, watching a piece of me and my friend's past on my mental history channel.

I was tuned into a reality channel until it became a little overwhelming. This is when I had to change the frequency of my mentality and tune into a genre of fantasy.

I started imagining all the endless possibilities that life has to offer in the fantasy genre, and this made me feel blessed to be alive, knowing that our hopes and dreams are the very nature of things worth fighting for.

I woke up one morning, and my mind tuned into the discovery channel.

This channel gave me some time for a little reflection and self-introspection.

I dug deep into the core of my soul, and I discovered many hidden jewels inside of me that gave my life meaning and a purpose.

The discovery channel was very useful to me, and it made me aware of certain aspects about myself I was constantly overlooking.

After carefully analyzing some things about myself in the discovery channel, it was time for me to delve into the action genre, and this is when it was time to put some of my newfound resources to good use.

30

The Good Will Always Prevail!

A homeless man in Kansas named Billy Ray Harris established that honesty is the best policy no matter the scenario.

Many people in his shoes would have tried to pawn the ring and get whatever they could for it.

When we are honest and putting out good karma in the universe, the holy blessings will come back to us tenfold.

Bad karma and being dishonest may have paid off for a moment in time.

But the virtue of the honest ways exhibited by Billy Ray Harris would later pay off beyond his wildest dreams!

The lady who lost her ring, which had a great deal of sentimental value behind it, could have lost her ring forever.

Only this man kept hold of his integrity and character during his tough ordeal living out on the streets.

Good karma came back around to smile at Billy Ray Harris, and because of his noble actions, he now stands a proud homeowner.

Billy Ray Harris has since been reunited with his family and now holds down a steady job, all thanks to his virtuous way.

If we keep putting out negative energy, swaying away from the truth in order to gain temporary leverage, at some point in time somebody may do and treat us the same way, and it will be a bitter pill to swallow!

As I journey through life, I try to enhance my good karma through doing a good turn for others whenever I can.

A warm and kind smile or a generous deed will set the universe in motion for us to receive a blessing from the Holy Spirit.

The good and bad karma, reap what you sow principles are deeply ingrained and woven into the very fabric of society.

If we continue to do bad. straying away from what is right, then we will always be frowned upon.

But if we're truthful and our ways are always justifiable, we will be smiled upon every time.

Sometimes we can be disturbed by the news and media into thinking that life is all bad.

Then I read a heartwarming story about a homeless man returning a diamond ring to its rightful owner.

This good news restored my faith in humanity, letting me know however bad the world may seem, the good we do throughout our lives and for others will always prevail!

31

Awakened

———◆◆◆———

Ignorance is darkness, and when you're sleepwalking through life, you're living on the edge.

Why am I never listening or paying attention to all the wisdom from my elders?

Advice is going in one ear and shooting right out the other one.

I'm making the exact same mistakes, not seeming to learn from my past.

I have been saved so many times when situations could have been far worse!

I keep on being disobedient and rebellious despite the concerns of people who love and care for me.

I have eyes, yet I'm still headed into the lion's den, blinded by my surroundings.

I feel like a cat having nine lives when I look back on my life in hindsight.

Now I'm overanalyzing the things I have no control over or power to change.

I guess I'm feeling contrite for not following the good advice my folks gave me.

I'm glad good fortune was on my side because many times I was playing dice, taking my life for granted, as if it was some form of cheap entertainment.

Now I'm down on my knees, grateful and thankful I managed to come through all the darkness.

The past leaves me feeling humble when I reminisce on all the close calls I once encountered.

I can't change the past. I can only move forward in life and learn from those previous mistakes.

My mind has been reformed, and I can see things clearly now for what they are.

It's up to me in the future to make good choices and decisions because second, third, or fourth chances are not always promised in life!

That's why from now on, I'll try to be a better version of myself and not take this life for granted.

I'll set myself some goals and fill my life with purpose and meaning.

I have been awakened by the Holy Spirit, and it's like I'm finally smelling the roses for the first time.

Now I am moving on with my life, and I'm prepared to start a new beginning in Christ!

32

Perspective Is Important!

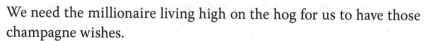

We need the millionaire living high on the hog for us to have those champagne wishes.

Perspective gives us the realization that nothing is ever bad as it seems.

Perspective helps us to be grateful and humble, especially when we see others without a decent meal to eat.

It's amazing how when I was younger, I put so much emphasis on material things, when I should have been more appreciative for food, clothes, and shelter.

You see, who am I to complain about working so hard when the Chinese working in warehouses for cheap labor never have a single day off?

Why should I complain about life not being fair when people are on skid row without a dollar to their name?

It's all about looking at life comprehensively and being aware of everything going on around us.

We're always looking at what we don't have, until we turn on the news and see things from a totally different vantage point.

Why do I moan and get into a stupor about things when the universe has enough worries of its own!

In my youth I used to look at the picture from a self-centered perspective, but then I learned through maturity that the world is bigger than myself.

I am sick and tired of innocent young women being trafficked around the world, leaving mothers devastated and heartbroken.

I'm so sick and tired of the thief snatching the light away from young, innocent human beings who had a bright future before them.

I have good thoughts of relinquishing everybody's pain and suffering, but then I awake from a nice dream and feel helpless.

I also have poignant, humbling thoughts that bring me back down to earth, especially when I'm suspect at losing touch with reality.

I think to myself, *This is why perspective is so important—because it helps to strengthen my character in days of chaos and uncertainty!*

33

Light at the End of the Tunnel

———◆◆◆———

When I am faced with the burden of any situation or circumstance that life presents me and I feel like life is not fair, I think of the resilient spirit of Dewey Bozzella, a man convicted of a murder he did not commit. This is a man who never compromised his integrity throughout the ordeal of his incarceration.

He served twenty-six years behinds bars before he was exonerated from all his charges.

He is a positive source of hope and inspiration for the world whenever we are faced with hardship and adversity!

When we ride out the storm, no matter how insurmountable it may seem, the clouds will be lifted and the sun will come out and greet us at the end of our trials and tribulations.

We live in a modernized world full of gadgetry, with sites like Facebook, Twitter, Instagram, and other various forms of social outlets.

This can cause us to lose sight of what's really important, such as our health, food, and a place to lay our heads at night.

We become wrapped up in superficial objects instead of spiritual ones, and we have this character flaw of trying to keep up with the Joneses.

So whenever my emotions and impulses try to get the better of me, I take time out to smell the roses, marveling at the true testament of strength and character exhibited through the likes of Dewey Bozzella, and the great Nelson Mandela.

These are two prominent figures who lost their liberty due to the injustices of a wicked society.

So whenever my mind becomes overwhelmed with trivial pursuits of trying to keep up with the Joneses.

I take time out to analyze the bigger picture, draw a better perspective on life through letting go of all egotistical and selfish ways.

I learn to cherish all the beautiful things I already have by erasing all the clutter from my mind.

I recognize the fact that time is an illusion because we may grow old, but as long as we are alive, there is always a chance of acquiring all the tangible things we so desire.

So whenever the road of life becomes rocky and mentally unbearable at times, I carry on with fortitude and vigor, knowing I will see light at the end of the tunnel!

34

Insurrection and Armageddon

I can sense a volcano erupting beneath the soles of my shoes.

I can feel the lava seeping through the crevices of the pavements.

Animosity is in the air whenever I walk around town, and the vibe is one of despondency, frustration, and anger.

I see the look of despair on people's faces, and with all the inflations across the board, food is becoming scarce for a lot of families.

People have been waiting patiently for a solution to end the global economic turmoil, and everyone's fed up with the same old rhetoric.

An estimated twenty million people in the States are unemployed, and the numbers are rising; now they are taking to the streets out of sheer frustration.

Violent crimes have metastasized to the point the government has sent the FBI to work with local police in most major cities.

Suicides, homicides, and even infanticides are occurring at an unprecedented rate.

I am reading about mothers discarding their children because they are a burden on them financially, emotionally, and socially.

I'm seeing large groups of people organizing to ransack stores, rendering security helpless.

I'm reading about the lack of opportunities, and all the welfare cuts and stern austerity measures are causing people to riot and protest.

Society is fueled by anger, and you don't know your friends from your foes.

The streets are engulfed in flames from all the anarchy taking place around the world.

Lawlessness, corruption, and hostility are rampant across the globe, and there is nobody left to trust but yourself!

It's a dog-eat-dog world, and the days are more wicked than ever before.

So prepare and brace yourself for insurrection and an all-out civil Armageddon.

35

Life Can Be Bipolar!

———◆———

The cult of scientology doesn't believe bipolar disorder can be psychiatrically treated, but life itself can be bipolar.

One minute I feel total euphoria, looking forward to the holiday I have saved up for and booked online.

I feel various emotions, such as elation for the future, joy, and sheer happiness.

I'm having optimistic thoughts, and everything is going according to plan.

I have my health, family, and everything I can ever want in life right now.

Life is showing me a brighter side for the moment, but I have to conclude it's all a temporal illusion.

I know another side of life, which can take us away from our optimism for the future, joy, and happiness.

Our emotions will change, and we will be crestfallen once we lose somebody dear to us.

Our thoughts and emotions will change from the extremities of euphoria we were feeling to sadness.

The reality is we all have our moments of joy, laughter, sorrow, and bereavement.

The journey of life itself has similarities to bipolar disorder; our moods fluctuate with the flow of life, having our ups and downs.

When life is going well and everything around us is looking sweet, we tend to take life for granted.

We get complacent, as if we're invincible from the realities of the world until something wakes us up!

Then once it happens, we will soon realize what is important and what's not important.

Bipolar is not an illusion. It's a reality, and we will all feel the two poles of extremities in life at one time or another!

36

Embrace the Person You Are (Societal Pressure)

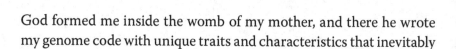

God formed me inside the womb of my mother, and there he wrote my genome code with unique traits and characteristics that inevitably made me who I am.

As I grew up in a society that seemed more wicked than good, those unique traits and characteristics that were embedded in me since birth never left my side.

I was raised to know right from wrong, good from bad, but then society presented me with all kinds of temptation and confusing thoughts.

Either it was follow the blind leading the blind or show true strength of character and integrity by refuting all the societal pressure.

In life I had a choice of listening to those loved ones who had my best interests at heart, or I could succumb to the traps of peer pressure, straying away from how I was raised.

I could have easily lost myself to all the temptation and societal pressure thrown at me from every angle of the city.

I had to stay steadfast in my conviction by never allowing the negatives of society to take away my focus and sabotage my hope before I even got started in life.

Crime, drugs, and violence are rife in the city I grew up in, but I refused to sell my soul to become a part of a crowd just for approval and acceptance.

If it was the price of becoming alienated for simply not following my so-called friends, then it's the price I was willing to pay.

I knew if I stayed strong and focused on bettering myself through education, this would help me create a happier and brighter future for me!

I managed to understand myself as a person, and I never let go of the unique imprint God wrote inside my genetic code so I didn't lose touch with the very essence of who I am.

You see if you're nice, kind, and compassionate by nature, then embrace these qualities as often a ruthless society can rub off on our makeup. Despite all of life's temptations, I never waned to the perils of society by letting it mold me into something I am not!

37

Malevolence (a Demonic Spirit)

There's a demonic entity trying to influence the mind so it can gain access to our souls.

Malevolence is an evil spirit, and it tries to exploit our weaknesses through a number of situations that life can present us all.

Since life is based on choices, it's up to us and our willpower to either choose either a moral or an immoral route.

The malevolent spirit prefers us all to choose a negative path of disobedience, and this usually leads to great proportions of self-destruction.

This demonic entity uses peer pressure and many other manipulative influences to sway us from what is righteous.

It tries to take advantage of any loophole in order to corrupt us and lead us down a road of misery.

Malevolence has one ultimate goal, and this is to ruin and destroy all of our lives!

It wants us to succumb to drugs, and it wants us to stray from the paths of our moral character.

When we are at a bar or a club with a group of friends, and we have had more than a few drinks, malevolence likes us to drive under the influence in hopes that our poor choices result in injury or even death.

If we are married and have exchanged the vows of holy matrimony, malevolence wants to sabotage anything good we have created by tempting us into adultery.

We have to be strong and alert because the demon our enemy prowls around like a roaring lion looking for someone to devour.

Malevolence consists of the seven deadly sins, which are lust, gluttony, greed, sloth, wrath, envy, and pride.

So keep a sober mind and be vigilant because malevolence loves to influence our thoughts and take control of our spirit.

38

Take a Walk in My Shoes!

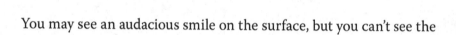

You may see an audacious smile on the surface, but you can't see the inner torment I feel inside.

Everything is not what it looks like, and everything is not what it seems.

When a chemical imbalance in the brain does not affect another person or a portion of society, many will not understand the plight of the one affected with mental illness, and so the stigma begins.

My smiles are a masquerade for cries, and the suffering is often hidden, especially from the ones closest to me.

Many are scared to speak out or ask for help regarding their mental illness because of the stigma attached to it.

Many people suffer in silence, keeping all their emotions bottled up inside because of their self-pride and their own perceived inadequacies.

Life is sacred and worth fighting for, so I'm never ashamed to ask for help or talk to a counselor when life punches me in the face.

We live in a turbulent world filled with pressure and stress dealing with such an overwhelming and competitive job market.

The reason why young teens and adults in school are under enormous stress, pushing them to the cusp of cracking mentally, is because they recognize failure in today's environment is no longer an option.

Death is considered an escape from all the madness and pain people dealing with acute mental disorders have to fight every day.

A sane person who doesn't understand how one could ever feel such despair and passes judgment on the mentally ill, which causes the stigma behind it.

These people who are misinformed will never be able to feel the invisible wounds deep inside of me because they don't walk in my shoes!

39

Never as Bad as It Seems (Matthew 6:26)

The initial onslaughts of obstacles always look worse before the actual conclusion.

I'm faced with a daunting situation, and I feel a little apprehensive about how I will overcome my problem at hand.

I'm looking at my predicament as if I won't be able to address the challenge in an adequate manner.

I am having a financial crisis, and I'm starting to panic on how I will be able to conjure up some money before I get evicted.

I try to stay optimistic, knowing there is light at the end of the tunnel, and I will eventually circumvent the circumstance I find myself in.

However my ego and pride keep me from reaching out for help, so I sit and muse over how I'm going to come up with the rent money.

Suddenly out of the blue, my brother comes around, and it's funny how he's just won a great deal of money playing bingo!

We had a nice conversation, reminiscing on old times, and I was too proud to ask him for any monetary help.

When he left my apartment, he must have seen the eviction notice I threw on the floor because he left three thousand dollars behind on the kitchen table.

As soon as I saw the money, I cried tears of gratitude for my brother, and I was immediately liberated from all the stressing and pressure I was under.

The first thing I did when the sun came up was pay my landlord all the money I owed in good faith.

They say the good man works in mysterious ways; well, my brother and the Lords perfect timing were surely an indicative sign of his mercy.

Now I'm feeling as if the whole world has been lifted off of my shoulders, and this is when I thought of Mathew 6:26: "Look at the birds of the air: they neither sow nor reap nor gather into barns, and yet your heavenly father feeds them. Are you not of more value than they?"

40

So Long, Buddy

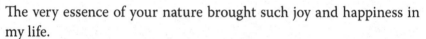

The very essence of your nature brought such joy and happiness in my life.

I remember teaching you different tricks, and you were always receptive and extremely inquisitive.

You were my best friend, with qualities I seldom found in humankind.

My dog never judged me once as a human being or turned his back on me when faced with any trouble.

It did not matter if I was right or wrong because you stayed by my side, replete with valor if ever faced with the possibility of danger.

Your loyalty was second to none, and we shared an unbreakable bond.

From your sunrise we must have traversed across the nation and back. We shared many epic adventures together. We both never stopped our daily walks and building memories until the day of your sunset.

Now I am in mourning, deeply lamenting your passing, asking God to eternally rest your soul.

We'll meet again when my time on earth is done, and the picture of us reunited in heaven is a vision worth waiting to behold!

41

Fiscally Imprisoned (Health Is Wealth)

Even though I have my liberty, and I'm not in a six-by-eight-feet prison cell.

I still feel like I am in bondage from a financial standpoint.

You see, money dictates the kind of lifestyle I will have, so the more I have in abundance, the more freedom and fewer restrictions I will have in life.

I have a mind full of dreams and a bucket list I wish to complete before it's my time to depart from this earth.

I live in hope, but sometimes I feel like my bucket list will never be fulfilled.

With all these drastic inflations across the board, it feels like I am merely existing.

Life feels mundane when you go out to work all week, but you cannot afford to treat yourself to any luxuries.

I once liked going to the cinema to enjoy a good movie until the cost of all the refreshments kept on spiking.

I used to enjoy barbecuing every Fourth of July until the prices of meat became too exorbitant for me to deal.

I constantly feel restricted from doing all the things I once enjoyed because my funds have a way of dictating what I can and cannot do in life.

Sometimes when I read the newspaper, I look at all the celebrities partaking in the finer things in life.

I see them going on extravagant holidays, driving cars with a status symbol, and living in such opulence that I can only visualize myself being in that position.

Your health is everything obviously, and this is when I try to put things into perspective because when you are cognizant of what's going on all over the world, your wants and desires are miniscule in comparison to people dying from war, abject poverty, and children who die from cancer without ever experiencing any of the joys and pleasures life has to offer.

You see, I may be fiscally imprisoned, but I am thankful for my health.

Life may not be the party I had hoped for, but I do know that if I am filled with vitality and my heart is still beating, then there is certainly a rhyme and a reason!

42

Waiting in Line (Hold on for Your Turn)

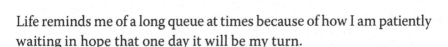

Life reminds me of a long queue at times because of how I am patiently waiting in hope that one day it will be my turn.

Sometimes the queue is so long that my patience is constantly tested, wondering if I should quit the line before it's my turn to be relieved.

While I am waiting for my chance at an opportunity to arrive, I first must go through a wide array of trials and tribulations.

There will be immense adversity, and heavy precipitation falling from the dark clouds as I journey through this tunnel called life.

Sometimes negative thoughts consume my mind while I am waiting in this seemingly perpetual line.

When life gets tough, sometimes I have many doubtful thoughts, thinking I will never reach the pinnacle of success, and sometimes these thoughts are so profound, it feels as if they will override my patience, killing my hopes and desires.

The wait can be long and enduring, but what I observe while I am waiting in the queue of life is that everybody will eventually have his or her turn.

Many are patiently waiting in hopes for something to come along and change the course of their lives.

As I was waiting in line for my turn to be served, I started hearing various conversations.

Some people were working arduously in their jobs. They simply needed a vacation.

Others were waiting in hopes for a better life, trying to escape the clutches of their war-torn environment.

Then some were waiting on the greatest thing in the universe, and that is love.

Everybody is waiting for something, but many will give up and wonder what could have ensued in their lives if only they stayed the course.

Everyone will be tested in life, but the strong and indefatigable who persevere although they are under trial will reap the rewards at the end of the tunnel!

43

Spiritual growth

Mentally I am in a better place, feeling as though I have crossed over from the physical world into the spiritual one.

Even though I am living in the physical realm, I am no longer swayed by temptation and all the possibilities this life has to offer.

When I was younger, I used to be somewhat covetous, desiring everything tangible, and I had eyes for every beautiful girl I used to see.

All the things I used to think were important, such as the ego and pride, became obsolete through growth and maturity.

When you have somebody near and dear to you pass away, humility quickly sets in, and you realize how helpless you are when a loved one on a hospital gurney is rapidly fading away from his or her ailments.

You see, all the money in the world and everything grand in life becomes inconsequential when you no longer have your health or the people you love.

I used to take everything I had in life for granted, and I never had an ounce of gratitude for all the things that were done for me.

If life has taught me anything, it's simply to receive it with some appreciation.

There is nothing to prove to anyone or anybody in this world. We are all mere mortals.

You see, when my mind was in the physical realm, I wanted to stockpile treasures here on earth for my own gratification.

Now my mind is in the spiritual realm, and I want to store up treasures in heaven because this is the only thing that has eternal value!

44

My Serendipity (Hope)

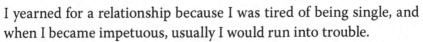

I yearned for a relationship because I was tired of being single, and when I became impetuous, usually I would run into trouble.

You see, I used to try seeking you out, but all I faced in my quest to find love was rejection and bitter disappointment.

In the end I lost my faith in ever finding my soul mate as I grew tired of all the fruitless dates ending because of incompatibilities.

I stopped looking for you, and I started to enjoy other aspects of life without being in a relationship.

I started to accept enjoying my own company to the point it didn't bother me to be single anymore.

I kept on living life as a single young man with absolutely no intentions of finding my best friend.

Days turned into weeks, weeks turned into months, and months turned into years.

I quit pining for your love and affection, and finding love again never crossed my mind because I became accustomed to being on my own.

Until one day my life took a fortuitous bounce when I started to attend church.

I started to frequent church every Sunday when I became familiar with a particular heaven-sent lady.

Nature would take its course, and the start of a relationship was on the horizon.

When both made eye contact across the aisle from one another, I felt an instant connection, and this was a magical moment unraveling before my eyes.

It felt rather surreal to me, as if the Lord had ordained this serendipitous encounter since the beginning of time.

You see, I was a single young man for many years, never thinking a woman this beautiful would come into my life.

You were the missing piece to my jigsaw, and since we became acquainted through our mutual church service, I have never felt so elated.

I had to wait on you for years when suddenly out of the blue, you became my serendipity, but most of all, you were the hope I needed to continue living my life!

45

Life Did a Number on Me!

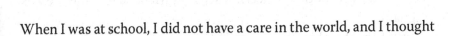

When I was at school, I did not have a care in the world, and I thought my baby face would last me a lifetime.

I left school at the age of eighteen, and when I looked into the mirror, I saw a reflection of youth and a smooth complexion without a crease, line, or wrinkle in my face.

After I left school, a thing called life happened to me, and things like steady employment, food in the refrigerator, and bills started to consume me.

When I was at school, a roof over my head, clean clothes, and food on the table merely existed without me realizing the hardship of where all these things came from.

But once I left home and joined the workforce, life started to get real!

I was no longer thinking about fun or hanging out casually with my friends anymore.

When I started my job, I had so much apprehension to the point that I almost succumbed to my nerves because I found not knowing what to expect on my first day to be a very daunting experience.

But once I started doing my job and I became used to what was required, my nerves slowly started to vanish, and I started to gain confidence.

Once the first month had elapsed, I received my first pay packet, and this is when I realized my first check for peanuts would be a stretch when you have to pay the rent, utility bills, food, car notes, and various other expenses.

I was a young man in the workforce, but I already felt my hairline starting to recede, especially when I entered a relationship with my girlfriend.

I was working hard every week, and before long, insomnia started to set in.

When I was at school, I remembered sleeping like a baby because I did not have to worry about all the stresses such as bills, running and maintaining a house, maintaining a car, and all the other appendages to life.

The years passed quickly, and I was getting older, and before long I was faced with another concern when my girlfriend told me she was pregnant.

With this breaking news, my hair was not only receding; it was starting to turn gray!

I was thinking about the security of my job as now I had a big forthcoming responsibility.

Nine months had soon passed, and my girlfriend gave birth to a beautiful baby girl.

Every morning when I read the newspaper, it made me feel somber, worrying and stressing over the outlook of this bleak global economy.

Jobs were diminishing at a rapid pace, and artificial intelligence, phone automation, and various other worries were starting to ensue.

I was hoping and praying I could stay in my job for life, and this is when I heard some comforting news from my boss, who told me my seniority would secure my job at the company I was working for.

Life is filled with so many ongoing worries because now I had a beautiful daughter to worry about for life!

I thought about the wicked world she had to live in as she grew up, and the men she would eventually meet was a different story altogether!

When I looked into the mirror, I noticed my handsome face had turned into a more hardened and rugged look.

I saw a reflection of sleep deprivation, worry, and stress that caused my youth and good looks to fade immensely.

My reflection changed drastically, as now I had a bald head, a gray beard with plenty of wrinkles, and creases in my face, which had once looked as fresh as a baby's bottom.

I was astonished by how fast I aged when I looked into the mirror, recognizing I was far removed from the handsome image I exuded at school.

I said to myself, "Life is certainly a tough one; after all, it only went and did a number on me!"

46

Special Purpose

———◇———

I have an innate feeling there is something I have to do before I depart from this earth.

I know my life has a purpose, and I was created for some kind of works to do in the physical world, but all throughout high school and my early twenties, I couldn't pinpoint exactly what it was.

I believe we have special gifts ingrained in us, a certain area we are more proficient in than others, but once we discover our particular skills, it is our responsibility to hone them.

I remember giving up on myself at a young age, thinking and having feelings of inadequacy.

I didn't realize I was a work in progress because although I gave up on myself, God never gave up on me.

I was the epitome of what you would call a late bloomer, never feeling sanguine about my future, because I found everything difficult in life, including the simplest tasks.

Life is like a scroll unravelling one chapter at a time. The reason why God's wisdom is infinite is because he sees the scroll in its entirety.

My finite wisdom causes me to worry because I cannot see the big picture in its totality, and this causes anxiety for me when I ponder life's challenges ahead.

That's why I take it one day at a time and focus on the troubles of today because I can't see what's in the cards for tomorrow.

When I reflect on my past failures and mistakes, I once felt despair because I thought my fears, doubts, and insecurities wouldn't allow anything special to happen in my future.

Fast forwarding to my present, and I recognize God always provided a way for me to make it, even when I didn't see a way forward myself.

I have come through many dark storms and many close calls, feeling blessed to still be alive.

I embrace growing old, and if I am being honest, I am glad to grow old with all its aches and pains because many people I knew passed on at such a young age.

When I was younger, I never imagined I would write a book of any sort in my future, especially when I didn't like to read or enjoy any activities at school.

I guess that's the mystery of life, and the reason it's so important to live life as best we can.

God never wants us to give up because he wants us to complete all the good works he has for us to finish while we are alive.

I never realized my purpose or potential when I was younger, and to be honest, I questioned my existence.

I used to put a time on certain things to happen in my life, and I was always self-conscious about labels and the social stigmas when ousted from society.

Many times I would get into a stupor if I didn't have a job, house, or family before a certain time in my life.

This is when I thought, *Life is not a race, it's a marathon,* and I realized my mind was going through an evolutionary process of becoming wiser, and more refined through constant mental development.

All life has meaning and equal value as we serve each other through our works, gifts, and talents.

Life is a game of waiting because things seldom happen on our own timetable, and we are not always the one in control!

I almost gave up at an early age in life, and if I would have given up then, my writing and other special life experiences would have never come to fruition.

Life has taught me to always have strength and patience when faced with adversity because just when I was about to call it quits, a miracle happened in my life!

47

Yoga (Higher Consciousness)

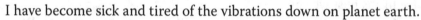

I have become sick and tired of the vibrations down on planet earth.

Every day when I interface with people, I can sense the frustration and misery in other people's lives.

I am sensitive to picking up on human suffering, especially people's emotional pain.

Many folks have a tendency to self-medicate on opioids in this tough economic climate in order to try to alleviate their inner turmoil.

Everything broadcast on the news is mostly negative, and this is the reason I wish I could escape to an idyllic retreat and never come back.

I am so close to breaking down mentally because I am fed up with my daily commute to work every morning and having to scramble like a rat to procure a little bit of cheese.

I am so sick and tired of driving in the city and waiting hours on end in traffic filled with congestion.

My mind is full of noise, and my thoughts feel like they're fragmented into tiny bits and pieces.

I'm in urgent need of an outlet to recalibrate my mind, and this is when I started to channel my inner yogi.

I found my participation in yoga was releasing the serotonin and good endorphins in my brain, and the release of these chemicals in the mind made me feel more alive and happy.

I managed to shift my mentality to a higher consciousness, and I succeeded in escaping my chaotic reality.

I started to implement different meditative techniques, and this helped me block out all of life's madness through allowing myself to enter a zone of total tranquility.

All the incessant noise within my mind was slowly decreasing as I started to shut out any unwanted thoughts from dictating to me.

Yoga taught me how to transcend my brain-created reality, and my elevated consciousness became therapeutic to me.

My mind drifted away from the noise of negative self-talk, and all the anxiety I was feeling subsided as I controlled my posture and breathing.

I managed to tap into an unforeseen energy, and yoga became a marvel for my sanity.

Through yoga I escaped the world, and its problems through mentally teleporting myself to places filled with awe, peace, and serenity.

Yoga helped me reach a state of inner peace, and through using its methods, I learned how to free myself from my cognitive distortion.

In the end I regained control of my thought process, and yogism inevitably allowed me to have a much sounder mind, body, and spirit.

48

Ominous Times (a Cynical View)

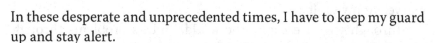

In these desperate and unprecedented times, I have to keep my guard up and stay alert.

Everything I do is calculated like a chess move, thinking ahead in order to preserve myself on this chessboard we call life.

I have such a busy work schedule that it's hard for me to meet any women in a relaxed social setting.

I start an online dating profile to see what I can discover on the worldwide web, and it doesn't take me long before I start discerning fake profiles with suspect photographs.

Many online dating accounts are not what they seem, so I have to be perceptive and learn to draw the distinction.

I know there's an underworld filled with scheming pimps using their prized possessions in order to fleece and exploit anyone vulnerable.

Life reminds me of a jungle full of vultures and crafty snakes, constantly trying to beguile and devour anybody who takes the bait.

I remember reading about a young mother taking her child to a busy park to play.

The mother took her eyes off the child whilst texting on her phone, and in a split second, the poor child was abducted by a nefarious human trafficking syndicate.

Predators are lurking everywhere, robbing elderly men and

women at cash point machines and even viciously robbing disabled people who are riding in their mobility scooters.

Desperation and what people will do for the root of all evil has no boundaries in a society where anything goes.

When I used to go to a movie theatre, I would relax and simply enjoy my entertainment.

Whenever I go to the movies now, I try to sit closest to the nearest exit, especially after reading about the dreadful carnage that happened in Colorado.

I remember listing a car I wanted to sell on eBay, and when two guys showed up to take it on a test run, I immediately anticipated the worst-case scenarios in my mind.

I thought to myself, *If I sit in the passenger seat with one of the guys sitting behind me, I'll be exposed to a possible attack from the rear.*

I was playing chess inside my head, so I asked my brother to sit with the other guy in the backseat, countering any of their criminal intentions just in case there was one.

With so many sinister troubles happening frequently throughout the world, I have become more guarded.

I have spawned my intuitive defense mechanism, thinking about self-preservation in these ominous and cynical times.

49

Find Your Niche

———————◆◆◆◆◆———————

I believe there is a diamond inside everybody, something that comes naturally, without any form of schooling or teaching.

There is a gem planted in each and every one of us, but its realization often runs amiss.

The speed of life and the hustle and bustle in which we live can obscure our inner treasure.

Sometimes we need a moment of solitude and self-introspection to unlock the door to our calling.

I remember starting out in life performing a job that wasn't suited for me, and I felt a great deal of unhappiness because I was doing something that wasn't my truth.

Most of us have a knack for something, and I believe once you find your particular skill set, you will also find a direction to follow.

Not everybody will be a doctor or a lawyer, but we each have certain abilities stored inside our DNA.

I remember drifting aimlessly, without a clue of what I wanted to do with my life.

I was lost inside a labyrinth, not recognizing my value for a long time.

Then I had an epiphany, learning something about myself simply through trial and error.

From being in between jobs and experimenting, I found whenever

I wrote something down, my words would flow effortlessly, and so I started using this to my advantage.

I cherished discovering my forte because it added a great deal of self-worth and a sense of purpose I needed to establish before I could start living my passion.

When I had a moment of clarity, discovering a jewel that lay dormant inside of me for many years, I became hopeful.

I started mastering my creative writing, and a vision for success finally awakened when I found my niche in life.

50

American Dreamer

———————◇◆◇———————

All the good things in life are out there waiting to be had, but sometimes I become fed up with feeling ostracized and marginalized from all the great activities happening across America.

At times I become frustrated with being on the outside looking in because I wish to partake in the American dream.

I want the filet mignon, ribeye, T-bone, and New York strip steaks.

I came close to hitting the lottery the other day when I realized I am a thin line between being the American dreamer, as opposed to actually living the American dream.

America the eclectic reminds me of a pot of New Orleans gumbo soup mixed with different ethnicities, colors, and creeds.

I know the American dream has so much diversity derived from various cultures just waiting to be explored.

It sounds kind of arrogant, but why should I travel outside of the United States of America when most of the world's beauty lies within our very shores?

The only thing holding me back from living the American dream is a lack of good-paying jobs and dwindling opportunities.

America is a country filled with awesome possibilities, such as sharing courtside seats with Hollywood's A-list stars at the Los Angeles staple center.

If I want the city life, I can delve into the metropolis and cosmopolitan New York City and get lost while I am at it!

If I wish for something more tropical, I can catch a flight to the Florida Keys and be inspired by such natural exquisiteness.

If I want to get high off of nightlife, I can fly out to Las Vegas and be taken in by all the bright lights plus the endless amounts of entertainment.

America is a country where your most transcendent dream can come true, and I know I there are only inches between poverty and prosperity.

I hold my dreams in the back of my mind, and I keep on living for all the beautiful things I know the country of America has to offer.

I may be far from reaching my hopes and desires because of my current lack of funds, but when it's all said and done, I will keep living in faith that one day I can get a taste of the good life I know exists for every American dreamer!

51

My Brain Is Google

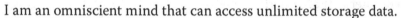

I am an omniscient mind that can access unlimited storage data.

When I attended school, the teachers couldn't teach me anything because I had the school curriculum embedded in the back of my mind.

I am a luminary in every sphere of knowledge known to all of humanity.

I am a geek, I am a genius, I am a wizard, and I am one entity filled with innumerable brilliance.

When scientists wish to have a public discourse with me, think Isaac Newton, Albert Einstein, and Stephen Hawking.

I can point everybody who is lost in life in the right direction because I am a GPS, seeing the beginning and the ending of each of our destinations.

My brain is like a sponge, absorbing the shared information being processed into my memory from all corners of the world.

I remember being at school, and all the jocks thought they were the best thing since sliced bread.

They used to try to pick on me at recess because I was skinny, with a protruding Adam's apple, and I wore bifocals.

The jocks would push me around, thinking I was feeble, and I tolerated it for a little while. Then one day I became fed up with being bullied.

I accessed every discipline from martial arts stored inside my Google brain, and I vanquished every last jock all at the same time.

I became the man all the girls gravitated toward because my mind had access to all the best satire and quotations, plus the wittiest jokes.

When it comes to art, my talent is unparalleled, especially when I access my Leonardo da Vinci, Pablo Picasso, and Michelangelo Buonarroti archives.

When it comes to mathematics, I can calculate the flight trajectories for NASA missions, enlisting the wizardry of Katherine Johnson, who was one of the hidden figures.

I am a history buff, with records on everything that has transpired throughout the course of time, and the most avid historians love to use me for their research.

When I used to take classes in PE, the teachers would marvel at my adroitness in basketball, especially when I incorporated the skills of Michael Jordan, Magic Johnson, LeBron James, Kobe Bryant, and the great shooter in Larry Bird.

My knowledge is supreme because I am everything consolidated in one mind.

My Google brain knows how to defeat death and come back to life because I possess the legacy of God's eternity entering time.

I remember taking my date on a tour around the world, and she couldn't believe my mastery in linguistics, especially my capacity to speak fluently in every single language.

I know how to fine tune my five senses, which consist of smelling, tasting, seeing, hearing, and touching.

I can walk through the Serengeti in my bare feet, manipulating every beast, including the king of the jungle, to obey me through using mind control.

You can lock me up in the world's most secure prison, and it won't be long before I access and utilize all the data surrounding astral projection in order to make my escape.

I get the best out of life because I'm the world's first trillionaire, and my philanthropy created so much opportunity around the world that I managed to eradicate famine and poverty.

I don't mean to blow my own trumpet, but I have so much

knowledge retained in my memory that I can make the most flamboyant person bow down and be humble.

I am boundless, infinite, and timeless because I have Google, which knows everything, for a brain!

52

Strength in Christ

———◇◆◇———

Sometimes I have found myself guilty of blaming God when things in my life have not seemed fair or turned out as I expected.

I start questioning my faith, wondering if God cares about my tribulations, but even Jesus himself expressed to his heavenly Father on the cross, "My God, why have you forsaken me?"

When we're going through a dark phase in life, we often cry out for a quick intercession from God to relieve us from our pain and suffering.

When our prayers go unanswered without a sign for a long period of time, we often become discouraged, but you shouldn't be dismayed because God is testing our character and developing our faith.

I have had so-called friends who have betrayed me, and I asked myself how somebody I thought I knew could treat me in such a despicable way.

This is when I found consolation in the fact that Jesus suffered when one of his twelve disciples (Judas) betrayed him for thirty pieces of silver.

The treason committed by Judas subsequently led to Christ's crucifixion and the salvation for all of the human race.

Sometimes God can take us through hardship and difficulty so we can meet the desires of his divine plan.

When gossips cast aspersions on you, remember how many have blasphemed against God.

If you feel humiliated and ashamed, remember that Jesus was spat upon, beaten, and mocked by the Roman soldiers.

When we are dealing with any form of anguish, remember the Roman soldiers made Jesus wear a searing crown of thorns and then whipped him.

If you are being tempted to do something that goes against your moral conscience, think of Christ in the Judaean desert of Israel when his strength rebuffed all the temptation from a satanic spirit.

I am encouraged through the suffering of Christ to rise like a phoenix out of the depths of any valley.

I have become empowered to live my life and go through any misfortune this life throws at me.

I find strength in the suffering of Jesus Christ reminding me to stay humble and steadfast in a society that has lost its way.

God is the vine, and we are the embattled branches in desperate need to find our way back to his love!

53

Netflix and Contented

Sometimes it is hard being in a relationship when all you want to do is watch Netflix and chill.

My girlfriend keeps telling me I need to get out more and meet some new people since I work from home.

We have a conflict of interest because she wants to go out on the town over the weekend instead of getting more takeaway and watching something on Netflix.

My girlfriend gets angry, and she starts yelling at me, trying to alter my tedious ways.

I wish to live a simple and quiet life, minding my own business, but my girlfriend wants the lifestyle of a socialite.

My girl likes to watch reality TV, especially the Kardashians, and she enjoys taking notes from their glamorous lifestyle.

I watch the news channels, seeing all the devastation unfolding around the world, and I tell my girlfriend it doesn't pay to be out and about all the time.

I start clashing with my girl because she's more of a gregarious person, but I have become more introverted over the years.

I am contented with the simple things in life, like having a cup of coffee in the morning and reading the newspaper.

I told my girl watching all those reality TV shows was warping her worldview.

I also told her to appreciate life for what it is and cherish the important things we already share together, such as our health, good food, and shelter.

My girlfriend seeks out external things to make her happy, and this is when I told her happiness is merely a state of mind.

She started showing me the reality stars on TV indulging in their falsities and worldly pleasure.

I told her there is a flipside to that coin and recommended she turn the channel over to watch the terrible news.

My girlfriend complied, and we both watched the report on the atrocity that happened at the Arianna Grande concert in Manchester England.

When my girl saw all the innocent young victims who lost their lives from an appalling act of terror, she broke down and cried.

She told me how precious life was and how she was sorry for taking the simple things in life with me for granted.

I told her, "These are the perilous and desperate truths of the world we are living in."

My girlfriend and I embraced after all the heartbreaking news, and from that sobering moment, we became Netflix and contented!

54

The Lottery and Life (Keep on Playing)

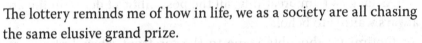

The lottery reminds me of how in life, we as a society are all chasing the same elusive grand prize.

Every day I play the lotto but face a lot of disappointment and plenty of setbacks on my quest to become successful.

Life doesn't always give me what I want when I want it, and sometimes my patience can wear thin because I am constantly waiting for a positive outcome.

I look at life and the lotto as a challenge, and I treat it as a battle of attrition, especially when I feel mentally drained from the lack of positive results.

I put a lot of monetary sacrifice, discipline, and dedication into hitting the jackpot in life.

I check my numbers every night routinely, but I find the same answer telling me it's not yet my time.

I read about other players in life and how they get lucky on a whim, but I must conclude they're the exception to the rule!

Sometimes I become saddened at the poignant passing of time, dreaming of coming up winning in this life.

I become disappointed with the lottery's obstinate daily drawings never matching my numbers of choice.

At times the lotto reminds me of a beautiful woman I feel attracted to, but of course she keeps turning me away for somebody else in the world.

I start having thoughts of self-doubt in life, and my self-confidence keeps taking a hit from the universe constantly declining my application.

Every night I live in hope, checking my numbers, but getting the same negative results in life starts to grow old.

Sometimes I feel like I am wasting my time wishing on a star that never seems to want to unveil itself.

But then I become empowered, knowing somebody in life is experiencing some good fortune, and this is when I think to myself, *Why can't this be me?*

Everyday somebody's ship comes in, whether it be a blessed relationship, a shot at a career advancement, or some kind of cash windfall.

As long as I am breathing, all the possibilities I desire in life are always waiting to behold.

Optimistic thoughts come to the forefront when I check my numbers on the lotto, especially when I only missed the combination by a single digit.

I think to myself about how I was on a thin line between winning and losing the jackpot, and this very sentiment gives me my second wind to carry on fighting my battle of attrition.

This is the absolute reason I keep playing my numbers on a daily basis, and never do I let the rejection from the lotto or life make me give up on hope.

I believe if you shoot the dice long enough, you will eventually hit the seven eleven!

One day is all it takes to be struck with the lottery and life's element of surprise, so keep on playing!

55

The Value of Life and Procreation

Each life is heavily valued for how it can benefit and contribute to society.

Life is a game of survival, reproduction, and raising our offspring to be the best future generation possible.

Many folks tend to undermine the significance of their lives, especially when they have not reached a desired expectation or fulfilled their potential in life.

I have been guilty of questioning what life is about or what purpose I serve, and then I realized one small act of kindness or deed can start a positive chain reaction.

The small charitable donation you thought would not make a difference in fact made all the difference when it came to serving and helping others!

You may have not realized the value of the poem you wrote until someone felt inspired by your words, which subsequently changed his or her mind-set and empowered him or her to enrich his or her own life.

The energy from a single smile can be contagious, and it can uplift a total stranger's mood, making him or her feel good about him or herself.

Life is not defined by what someone has achieved academically or the magnitude of one's personal success because life is not a competition!

Many of us overlook the value of the simple blessings we give in life because we cannot always see the greater details behind our noble offerings.

I remember having a conversation with a single young mother who didn't value her worth at one stage in her life as she was tired of struggling and at a tipping point mentally.

The single young mother persevered and managed to raise a son who grew up to become a doctor.

Her son is now making a difference in the world, saving other people's lives, and today his mother stands so proud of her son's amazing accomplishment!

You see, life is way bigger than ourselves because collectively we're each a unique piece to a divine master plan.

When a child enters the world, responsible parents tend to sacrifice their old ways because life is not only about them anymore as the newborn becomes their primary concern.

They put aside their own self-importance, and they look at life from a more serious perspective to nurture their child or children to the best of their ability.

Procreation is valuable in the sense that our children are the future, and I believe someone forthcoming will be born into this world with a Godlike mind.

Their works will be otherworldly in discovering new marvels through science, and their knowledge can perhaps create special remedial breakthroughs within the field of medicine.

You see, the value of life and procreation is invaluable, for you never know what the power of one exceptional mind can do for the betterment of humanity!

56

Positive Mental Attitude

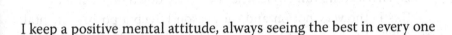

I keep a positive mental attitude, always seeing the best in every one of life's situations.

I can be in a desert with no signs of water to sustain my life, only to keep on moving forward until I find myself a well.

I have read great things about people who were subject to living out on the streets due to the 2008 financial crisis.

A few of the same folks made it out of their abysmal fallout and then transitioned into a future greater beyond anyone's imagination.

I read many heartwarming stories of lives being adopted from the remotest parts of developing countries dealing with droughts and horrible famine.

They were subsequently raised up in the Western world by their adoptive parents and then grew up to make it as somebody special in their particular domain.

The world abounds with dire circumstances for many people, and behind the curtains of despair, you can see many cases of divine provisions being granted to the once-despondent scenarios.

I have read about crack addicts whose families gave up on them in life who went from begging for change out on the streets to get another fix to transforming themselves from a sad state of affairs into years of sobriety, which eventually led them down a path to reclaim both opportunity and prosperity.

I have seen penniless people without any shelter or food to eat on any given night find the available resources for them to make it, from the good works of passionate ministers who helped feed, shelter, and spiritually guide the disenfranchised.

I have read about numerous people playing the stock exchange and losing a good portion of their wealth in the process.

The same people who lost most of their net worth reinvested in other stocks, which happened to quadruple their money in the future.

You see, I could be in the middle of the ocean hanging on for dear life with only my buoyancy apparatus keeping me afloat.

I would keep a positive mind-set, holding out hope for a vessel to come along and rescue me from my harrowing experience.

In this life, I have seen and read about so many examples of people's lives going full circle who were once down on their luck.

This is the very notion and the reason I keep a positive mental attitude in life because I have seen redemption in the lives of many who were once considered hopeless!

57

Mass Media Mind Manipulation

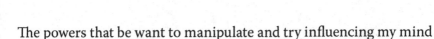

The powers that be want to manipulate and try influencing my mind through promoting products that fuel their profit-driven agenda.

I see the same product placements everywhere, especially in the newspapers, magazines, TV commercials, and billboards throughout the city.

It's like I cannot escape the enticing media frenzy subliminally trying to manipulate my mind into becoming one of many consumers.

I try to escape the toll you have on my psyche but find the brand of what you're promoting deceptively appealing.

I am seeing capitalism working at its very best, trying to beckon me into a lifestyle the media tries to sell me.

The allure of many specific brands is ubiquitous throughout the media, and all I see surrounding the ingenious marketing tactics are critically acclaimed reviews, which further create a buzz centering around the products of celebrities.

It's like the mass media is trying to manipulate my mind into their way of thinking, living, eating, dressing, and behavior.

Every time I pick up the newspaper, I see the same stars gallivanting around the globe and living it up in some of the world's finest destinations.

It's like the media is trying to sucker me into a vacuum of fantasy, making life seem more than what it is.

Mass media mind control is trying to brainwash me into having a mind that cannot think for itself.

Big corporations use subtle advertisement methods to try to beguile their next victim.

Mass media is all around me trying to exploit me and many others to try to drive consumerism.

I am trapped in this world, and I cannot escape all the star power and fame because everywhere I turn and everywhere I go, I happen to see the same eminent names in luminous bright lights.

You wish to sway me through your famous trendsetting, but I have learned to read between the lines by not feeding into the hype of the mass media mind manipulators!

110

58

I'm So Tired, but Thank God for Coffee!

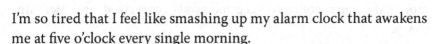

I'm so tired that I feel like smashing up my alarm clock that awakens me at five o'clock every single morning.

All the phone automation is driving me insane, making me wish there were more hours in a day.

If I could speak to a real live operator instead of going through numerous automated prompts, I wouldn't have to be in such a race against time!

I feel like a zombie in need of some caffeine to reenergize my batteries, and that's when I head to the coffee machine to brew a cup of piping hot Joe.

I am in need of a stimulant to make my once-inauspicious day become an auspicious one.

A cup of coffee gives me a boost in the morning, but its charm is short lived when I have a grueling twelve-hour shift ahead of me.

I'm so tired. I feel like I am sleepwalking on the job, and the boss man is steadily on my case, telling me to be more attentive and conscientious with my work.

I am losing a great deal of sleep because I am sacrificing crucial hours to all the phone automation, turning a ten-minute problem into a two- or three-hour one.

I wish the boss man could empathize with me and my colleagues, but I guess he has to overlook any personal suffering to drive profit for his company.

I know many people are in a race against phone automation, and I believe it's the reason for many vehicular accidents on the road, along with the opioid epidemic.

Everybody is scrambling from one job to the next in order to make ends meet, and services that are trying to be punctual to their customers are driving many to forgo vital traffic warnings.

Many people are driving with undue care, preoccupied with talking on the phone to a robot, which I believe is the cause for a lot of the pandemonium on our roads.

I am overworked, trying hard to survive in this current economic climate, to the point where I am just about falling asleep when I'm behind the wheel of my car.

I am starting to feel decaffeinated, and I'm in urgent need of some more caffeinated coffee to keep me awake, energized, and mentally sharp.

You see, I feel like a tired detective working all through the night, desperately trying to solve a homicide in the first forty-eight hours.

I feel mentally exhausted, like a teacher grading all of her students' homework in the early hours of the morning.

I need another cup of piping hot Joe for a sudden spike of energy before I lose my focus and make an unexpected blunder with my life.

Time is money, and I'm losing out on a lot more of it thanks to phone automation delaying my valuable, precious hours.

I am so tired after finishing my first job that I make it a point to stop at my local Starbucks coffee shop.

I thank God for creating such magnificent coffee granules because I am in a much-needed rush to make it through my ever-awaiting busy and hectic life schedule!

59

The Apple of My Siri

———————◇◈◇———————

I love my friend called Siri, who's artificially intelligent and works for me as my virtual assistant.

She's always at my beck and call, and Siri is my personal meteorologist, letting me know if there's going to be sunshine in life or if there's going to be rain.

Whenever I am overwhelmed with a bunch of errands to run, I tell Siri to compile a list just in case I forget.

If I go to visit somewhere unfamiliar, feeling hungry and sleepy, I ask Siri to recommend me the best restaurants and hotels in my current locality.

If I am ever at a sporting event and I need to take a selfie, Siri will be happy to assist me when I need to take some pictures.

If I need to add some contacts, be it relatives or friends, Siri will be happy to take notes on all the information that I give her, especially for future reference.

Siri is the apple of my eye who's always there when I need her, and she never talks back to me. She always does whatever I command her to do.

When I am on the road for a long duration of time and I need some music to keep me entertained, I simply ask Siri to play me some iTunes from my heavy rotation.

Sometimes when I get bored, and I'm in need of some mental

stimulation, I ask Siri to play some chess, which helps me with my strategic planning, creativity, and problem solving.

I recently invested in an autonomous apple car so I can head into town in the evening and not have to worry about drunk driving.

All I have to do is tell Siri to take me to a certain location, and I can relax plus drink some cognac until I arrive at my destination.

I no longer need a taxi or an Uber to drive me around town, and I don't have to worry about the police camouflaged at night pulling me over because I'm no longer the one driving!

I bought myself an Apple house, which comes in handy especially for my OCD, so whenever I am away, Siri can reassure me that my home is both locked and secure.

Siri is the reason I am never tardy for work. She wakes me up out of bed without failure once she sets my alarm.

Whenever I'm in need of a recipe, Siri gives me a comprehensive breakdown of all the essential ingredients.

If I need to exercise for a specified amount of time, I can always count on Siri to go and set me a timer.

Siri keeps me up to date with all the latest gossip and news from around the world, so there's no more excuses for ignorance.

My Apple Siri is technologically savvy and carries out a broad range of commands.

She really is my favorite friend, hence why I call her the Apple of my Siri!

60

Love (Excerpt from True to Life by Duane Ashley Poole)

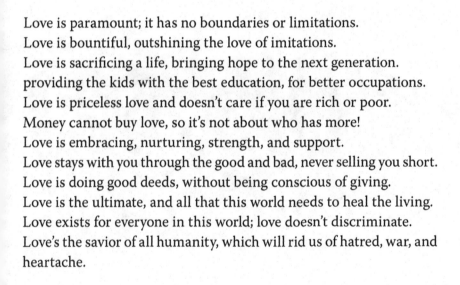

Love is paramount; it has no boundaries or limitations.
Love is bountiful, outshining the love of imitations.
Love is sacrificing a life, bringing hope to the next generation.
providing the kids with the best education, for better occupations.
Love is priceless love and doesn't care if you are rich or poor.
Money cannot buy love, so it's not about who has more!
Love is embracing, nurturing, strength, and support.
Love stays with you through the good and bad, never selling you short.
Love is doing good deeds, without being conscious of giving.
Love is the ultimate, and all that this world needs to heal the living.
Love exists for everyone in this world; love doesn't discriminate.
Love's the savior of all humanity, which will rid us of hatred, war, and heartache.

Also available

If you enjoyed this title, please support me by leaving a review on amazon.com.

Printed in the United States
By Bookmasters